A Key to Loving

Before she became a Bahá'í, Betty Frost worked as a flight officer for the Canadian Airforce in the Intelligence Section, where one of her postings was to the War Room in Ottawa. Later she began a serious study of the Bahá'í Teachings on human relationships and individual development and has taught courses on the subject to students of many different ages and backgrounds.

She served for sixteen years as a volunteer at the Bahá'í World Centre, most recently as Secretary-Aide to a member of the Universal House of Justice, the Supreme Council of the Bahá'í Faith; she also served as the first Secretary-Aide to the International Teaching Centre.

Mrs Frost is the mother of three, and the grandmother of eight children.

A Key to Loving

by

Betty Frost

GEORGE RONALD

OXFORD

GEORGE RONALD, Publisher
46 High Street, Kidlington, Oxford OX5 2DN

A Cataloguing-in-Publishing entry is available from the
British Library

ISBN 0-85398-380-1

Printed in Great Britain by The Cromwell Press
Broughton Gifford, Wiltshire

Contents

1 The most important feat 1

2 Our reaction of hurt and anger 5

3 Spiritual law and physical law 9

4 What we think others feel about us 13

5 How we feel about others 26

6 How we act towards others 36

7 Dependence on love 45

8 Reinforcement is needed 55

I

The most important feat

In the early part of this century a remarkable figure made the following pronouncement: 'The most important feat in this day is harmony and agreement.'[1]

It is not very difficult to perceive the importance of 'harmony and agreement' when we look at the world at large with its conflicts, wars, border disputes and religious squabbles, together with the ever-growing problem of air and water pollution which sees no borders. It is not even difficult to see the attainment of peaceful settlements in war zones and amicable agreements as regards poisonous emissions as a kind of 'feat', even though this is a word which one usually thinks of in relation to climbing Mount Everest or landing on the moon.

But what about our own relationships? We can look at the reported rising divorce rates, the fearful family disputes which sometimes even lead to violence, and become aware of the very great importance of achieving 'harmony and agreement', and the great effort involved in so doing. And if these statistics haven't touched us personally, we can look much closer to home. Why is it so difficult to maintain a loving, creative relationship with the single person we have chosen as a life partner – or even to maintain a harmonious relationship with our own family or those with whom we work?

Or, to put it in very simple language, why is it such a 'feat' to be able to love? There is no doubt that we would like to have this ability (if only other people were a little more lovable!). And there is no doubt that from whatever religious background we come, the teaching of love has been at the root and core of our religion.

It is not only religious leaders who summon us to achieve 'harmony and agreement'. In the world of business, professional counsellors are paid high returns for their ability to settle problems among workers. Management jobs often go to those whose ability has been proven in being able to 'get along' with their co-workers. And how many family counsellors, psychiatrists and psychologists are called in by war-weary couples to try to assist them in achieving a better relationship?

We quote, once again, from that 'remarkable figure' mentioned in the opening sentence (who was 'Abdu'l-Bahá, son of the Founder of the

Bahá'í Faith), '. . . order your lives in accordance with the first principle of the divine teaching, which is love'.[2]

He also said: 'In the world of existence there is no more powerful magnet than the magnet of love.'[3]

If it is the 'first principle of the divine teaching' and a 'powerful magnet', why is the achievement of a loving relationship, so deeply desired by so many of us, such a difficult task? Perhaps one needs to look at the causes of our feelings of anger and hurt.

It should be noted that some of those feelings may arise from very serious actions on the part of others – actions which may even require that legal steps be taken or that psychiatric guidance be sought, or that the person involved, in the case of a battered wife, seek some safe haven. It is not proposed to deal, except in a general way, with this kind of problem.

What will be examined are those things which result in what might be termed 'family rows', which gradually erode a relationship. . . the kind of arguments which can change what was once considered a 'marriage made in heaven' to a battleground. Of course battlegrounds can exist in places other than in a marriage. The workplace, the school, the family, and even the local community can also be places where hurt feelings, anger and resentment can fester.

Having experienced such problems, particularly

in my early life, I was impelled to study the
Writings of the Bahá'í Faith to see if there was
some clue as to how one could overcome the
seemingly natural response of anger and hurt. The
pages which follow outline the spiritual principles
and laws which I have personally found to be of
enormous help in understanding negative reactions
and in learning the spiritual principles which
gradually help to overcome them.

2

Our reaction of hurt and anger

The key word in this concept is 'reaction'. Although it may seem that we are taking 'action' to defend or justify ourselves in a family quarrel, for the most part, the things which we do or say are a direct result of our 'reaction' to hurt and/or anger which we feel has been caused by the other person. It would appear to me that there are two sides to this 'reaction'.

(1) What we think the *other person feels* about us, which is apparent because of what he/she says or does. (*their* judgment)

(2) What *we feel* about the other person because of what he/she says or does. (*our* judgment)

Here are some examples:
The other person does something which is

hurtful to us: or they claim we have done something to hurt them. The instant reaction is to defend ourselves: 'You make me furious.' 'You make me sick!' 'He/she makes me tired.' If we are making such comments, the implication is that we have signed over our sense of well-being to another human being. If it is the other person who makes such statements, it would seem likely that we have done something (however unintentionally) which has caused anguish, and our usual reaction is to rush to our own defence.

Sometimes it seems that our motives are misjudged. There is nothing more hurtful than to have someone claim we have acted out of self-interest when, in our opinion, whatever action we took was an unselfish one. The usual reaction is to feel a deep sense of hurt that anyone, especially someone near and dear to us, could feel this way about us. On the other hand, we may be the one who is misjudging. It is all too easy to assume that other people act out of spite, jealousy and a sense of superiority. Our reaction in this case is usually one of anger.

They claim we haven't lived up to their standards or wishes. This can sometimes happen if we choose to follow a different religion; or perhaps (in the other person's opinion) we have not lived up to their standards or the standards of the particular Faith we practise. The customary reaction is one of defence, probably coupled with feelings of hurt. From our side, we may feel that the other person has failed miserably to live up to the lofty standards we have set for them. Our sense of betrayal causes an angry reaction.

As will be seen by the foregoing examples, there are many times in which we become either hurt or angry (or both) because of **what we think others feel about us** and because of **what we feel about them**.

In each case there is what might be termed a 'passive response'. We have not actively tried to understand either our own behaviour or that of the other person. We have merely 'reacted'. Can we think of instances in our own lives where this is what happened?

Our reactions may not be verbal. Quite often, either because of our upbringing which may frown upon an open exchange of anger, or because we may be consciously trying to 'get along' with the other person, the reaction is something we merely feel. But, unfortunately, the feeling is what ultimately gets across to the other person.

Many years ago when the British were leaving one of the outposts of their far-flung Empire, one of the officers asked a native why he was so happy at their departure. 'Haven't we always treated you well? Haven't we created schools and even Universities for you? Have we ever treated you badly?' The native thought for a moment, and then said that all of these things were true, but what bothered him was 'the way you looked at us'.

We don't have to travel that far, however, to be aware of the fact that the same comment made to two different people can have very different connotations. For example, after eating a rather mediocre meal we may say, rather perfunctorily, to our hostess: 'Thank you for the delicious dinner.' Contrast the feeling accompanying the same statement, following an equally mediocre meal which has been cooked for the first time by one's twelve-year-old daughter!

Perhaps one of the most important lessons one can learn about reaction to other people is that it is what we **feel** that gets across.

One might say: 'It is all very well to say that we shouldn't have negative feelings about another individual. But if you heard what he/she said the other evening, you'd feel as angry as I did!'

This is our common justification. What we hope to do in this small presentation is to suggest that there are ways in which we can begin to overcome the inertia of simply responding to the annoying behaviour of another. The reader should be warned that it will probably take a considerable period of time, may result in numerous failures, and will demand a selflessness which may almost amount to 'heroism', in order to achieve the desired result. But in life we have to either go forward or backward.

3

Spiritual law and physical law

In the nineteenth century the following statement was made by Bahá'u'lláh, Founder of the Bahá'í Faith: 'The fundamental purpose animating the Faith of God and His Religion is to safeguard the interests and promote the unity of the human race, and to foster the spirit of love and fellowship amongst men.'[1]

Since a fundamental purpose of the Faith of God is to 'foster the spirit of love and fellowship' does it not seem logical that some kind of spiritual laws would be given which would help us to achieve this desirable condition? It is all very well to say to someone that they should be loving – a just God would surely supply some means by which it could be achieved.

We don't usually think of spiritual laws as

anything but a sort of 'guidance' given to us in the various Holy Books which we can accept or reject as we see fit. It normally doesn't occur to us that spiritual law could be equated with physical law. But if we look at the tone of authority with which such divine guidance is given, there is no question that it is, in reality, a spiritual law. Bahá'u'lláh did not say – 'it would be desirable if', 'it is suggested that' or even 'you would be happier if you'. He spoke in a majestic tone, later to be reflected in the Words of 'Abdu'l-Bahá: 'Order your lives in accordance with the first principle of divine guidance which is love.'

Let us look for a moment at physical laws. If God created the universe did He not also create physical laws? No one really questions physical laws. If we are painting the roof of the house and the ladder slips, we may reasonably expect to have at least a broken leg. One doesn't question the law of gravity. If we turn on an electric switch, are we surprised when the room is flooded with light? (Conversely, if we put our hand into an electric socket, we would expect to be shocked at the result!) We have come to expect the wonderful results which are occurring so rapidly in this century because of the ever-advancing knowledge and use of physical laws in the field of communication. The use of a computer demands rigid attention to detail; but when it is followed, the results are almost miraculous.

We are becoming increasingly aware of not only

the laws of physics, but the laws of nature on which 'our fragile planet' depends.

If this world is not just a chance happening, we must assume that God made laws which rule our physical lives and the life of the planet. Does it not seem logical that He also created spiritual laws which are just as immutable? Would it not seem reasonable to suppose that obedience to spiritual laws would bring about a sense of joy, and that disobedience to them would bring about the opposite? Bahá'u'lláh, the most recent Manifestation of God, stated: 'Whoso keepeth the commandments of God shall attain everlasting felicity.'[2]

Bahá'u'lláh made a very interesting comment concerning laws. He said: 'Think not that We have revealed unto you a mere code of laws. Nay, rather, We have unsealed the choice wine with the fingers of might and power.'[3] If wine is 'unsealed' it must first have had to be put in the bottle. It would certainly seem that the spiritual laws were, therefore, not given to mankind as an afterthought. They have always been in existence. In this particular era we have been more greatly endowed because, just as in every religious Dispensation, special laws have been revealed which are pertinent to this particular time in history. Secondly, the spiritual laws which never really change concerning the relationship of individuals have been given to us with greater clarity. Perhaps it is because in this era we have to not only bring about love and unity between individuals, but on a world scale.

'Know assuredly that My commandments are the lamps of My loving providence among My servants, and the keys of My mercy for My creatures', Bahá'u'lláh stated.[4] It is interesting to note that He used the analogies of 'lamps' and 'keys' to refer to His laws. Can these perhaps be perceived as signifying the shedding of light and the opening of doors to our understanding?

4

What we think others feel about us

Before studying the question of spiritual law there are two points which need to be stressed. The first is that spiritual laws apply to us as individuals. We cannot impose spiritual laws upon anyone else. (It doesn't help to say that our problems stem from the fact that so-and-so doesn't understand us.) The second point is that even if we succeed in following spiritual law, it is not guaranteed that this will bring about a loving relationship. However, it is very likely that the relationship will improve, simply because we are not adding to the problem and, in fact, are perceiving the causes behind it. In the event that the other person in the relationship does not respond, the important thing is that we will not become bitter, and that we will find an inner peace of mind and a sense of joy which the most difficult adversary cannot eradicate.

In now considering the question of 'what we think others feel about us', a question we might pose to ourselves is this: In the past year how many times have we *deliberately* done something to hurt another person? On the other hand, in the past year how many times have we felt hurt, especially when it seems that the other person is *deliberately* doing something to hurt us? Almost inevitably the number of occasions rises dramatically as one answers the second question. Why is this so?

The answer is pretty obvious. We have allowed another person to judge us. We have accepted their judgment of whatever we have done, even when we feel we have been terribly misjudged. This is in direct violation of a very important spiritual law which was revealed by Bahá'u'lláh well over a hundred years ago: 'Set before thine eyes God's unerring Balance and, as one standing in His Presence, weigh in that Balance thine actions every day, every moment of thy life.'[1]

'Trust in God, and be unmoved by either praise or false accusations. . . depend entirely on God,'[2] 'Abdu'l-Bahá counselled.

If we take this spiritual law seriously, the power of another individual to shatter our sense of self-esteem disappears. Instead of being wounded by the unjust accusations or comments of another person (which may have been said in a moment of anger), we look towards the judgment of God. This has a very calming effect, and it enables us to become more detached from the situation.

There is a very interesting story told about the Buddha, who responded to a follower who had come to him saying that he had been deeply hurt by another. The Buddha asked him to whom a gift would belong if the recipient refused to accept it. The puzzled follower replied that it would, of course, belong to the person who had presented it. 'Just so,' replied the Buddha.

In other words, if we do not accept harsh comments made by another person, these unkind words remain with the person who said them.

It is hardly necessary to state that if we are able to consciously accept the spiritual law that God is our Judge, our standards are necessarily raised. In this context, we have to take a closer look at the spiritual law mentioned above which states that we should be 'unmoved by either praise or false accusations. . .' It is interesting to note that the word 'false' is included here. Obviously, if the accusations are true (or even slightly true), we should not remain 'unmoved'.

One's usual reaction to harsh words is to either deny them, justify our actions, or accuse the other person. If one could take a moment to 'act' instead of 'reacting', it might be possible to see whether or not the accusation is justified – or perhaps, slightly justified. Sometimes the hurt or anger is so great we are in no condition to think logically. It may be necessary to take the 'action' of remaining quiet for the moment, inwardly saying prayers for tranquillity and strength.

The spiritual law which is applicable in determining whether or not the accusation is justified is that of truthfulness. 'Abdu'l-Bahá said: 'Truthfulness is the foundation of all human virtues. Without truthfulness, progress and success, in all the worlds of God, are impossible for any soul. When this holy attribute is established in man, all the divine qualities will also be acquired.'[3]

This appears to be a very remarkable spiritual law. When we learn to be truthful, all of the 'divine qualities' will be acquired. It might be helpful to consider the case of an alcoholic. It is a generally accepted fact that an alcoholic cannot overcome his addiction unless he personally admits that there is a problem. Would this not also be true of what might be considered as less serious problems in our behaviour? Once we are able to accept the fact that we have been discourteous, unthoughtful, self-motivated (or whatever), we are in a position to begin to acquire the 'divine qualities' mentioned above. But if we don't recognize where we have failed, how can we begin to progress?

Bahá'u'lláh said that through the Teachings of God '. . .every man will advance and develop until he attaineth the station at which he can manifest all the potential forces with which his inmost true self hath been endowed'.[4] There is no doubt that most of us would like to manifest all of the potential we've been given. Sometimes we find out, to our dismay, where we are going wrong. When someone makes an unflattering statement, we are cut to the quick.

It is an interesting commentary on human behaviour that when we wish to develop our full potential as a golfer, we will pay a golf pro a large amount of money to point out our faults!

But it is, without doubt, a very daunting task to face up to our own personal imperfections. Our sense of self-worth is very fragile at times, and it can be shattering to see where we have failed. It is probably for this reason that we defend ourselves with such vehemence. A cautionary note should be struck in this regard, that although we must try to be truthful with ourselves, we should be *just* to ourselves, and not feel a sense of guilt about something we either didn't do or were un-conscious of doing. Many people feel guilty about the actions of others, especially their children. Bahá'u'lláh said: 'Be fair to yourselves and to others, that the evidence of justice may be revealed through your deeds among Our faithful servants.'[5]

Often, the criticism is about something which, in retrospect, is quite inconsequential. However, when there are basic difficulties between two people, a negative comment, even about food, can be interpreted as a character attack. Here is an example: a close relative of mine was having marital problems and on one rather memorable occasion she had prepared a delicious dinner, serving it buffet style. Her husband put some broccoli on his plate, but made several snide comments about it including the fact that he couldn't understand why his wife had to serve it at practically every meal. As the 'broccolian' comments continued, it was obvious that the wife was getting more angry by the minute. Finally, in a moment of extreme provocation, she seized her husband's plate with some vigor, and scooped the offending broccoli back into the serving dish. Needless to say, the atmosphere didn't improve!

In thinking about the situation and how it could have been handled using spiritual law, the wife could have realized, initially, that the husband was not her judge. This would have calmed her sufficiently to look more logically at the comments, and realize that perhaps she did serve broccoli quite frequently. She might have nipped the source of argument in the bud by agreeing, and suggesting a compromise. She would make a point of always serving a second vegetable so that he could eat the broccoli if he so wished, or leave it. She might even add a touch of humour to her admission by suggesting she was a bit of a 'broccoli freak'. There is nothing more deflating to a budding argument, than to agree.

On the other hand it should not be assumed that the preservation of relationships is the responsibility of the woman alone. Ideally, both sides will wish to be aware of, and obedient to spiritual laws. For example, in the above situation the husband's initial annoyance at seeing the inevitable broccoli might have been softened if he had consciously thought about the law of seeing the good points in another individual (see p. 30). He could have concentrated on the loving service his wife had rendered in the preparation of such an otherwise delicious meal. He might also have called to mind the spiritual law which states that '. . .if you wish to give admonition or advice let it be offered in such a way that it will not burden the receiver' (see p. 24). Other spiritual laws concerning such situations appear in the chapter 'How we act towards others'.

This does not mean to imply that the basic marital difficulty is resolved. But the more arguments and fights that can be avoided, the less harsh words are exchanged. We have been advised that the tongue is a 'smouldering fire' and excess of speech a 'deadly poison'. Each argument adds fuel to that fire.

Even being aware of spiritual law, it is easy to fall into the trap of 'reaction'. (Just ask me!) But when we fail, so to speak, in a situation such as the one described above, a positive result can occur if we subsequently try to consciously figure out the spiritual law which should have been followed. It will help us to understand ourselves, and make it easier to be aware of spiritual law on future occasions. If, however, we don't use that opportunity of 'failure' to learn something, we simply reinforce our feelings of animosity.

Sometimes the actual comments and criticisms are of a more personal and serious nature. One of the most helpful, but simple statements on this subject was made by Amatu'l-Bahá Rúḥíyyih Khánum in her book *Prescription for Living*. She indicated that we weren't expected to 'issue forth with wings, halo and harp overnight'. If we had been expected to do so, why were there so many prayers revealed for forgiveness? One example is the following portion of a prayer revealed by 'Abdu'l-Bahá:

> . . .We are all sinners, and Thou art the Forgiver of sins, the Merciful, the Compassionate. O Lord! Look not at our shortcomings. Deal with us according to Thy grace and bounty. Our shortcomings are many, but the ocean of Thy forgiveness is boundless. Our weakness is grievous, but the evidence of Thine aid and assistance are clear. Therefore, confirm and strengthen us. . .[6]

Someone once likened the acceptance of forgiveness to the feeling which a prisoner would have who had been confined to a dark and narrow cell for years and suddenly found himself outside the prison in the midst of beautiful trees, flowers and sunshine.

If prayers are revealed promising forgiveness, this must also be a spiritual law. Of course, one must recognize one's shortcomings, and be willing to try to make things right. Undoubtedly there are some occasions when one cannot make things right. However, God has promised forgiveness, even for the most 'grievous' of weaknesses. Many of the sins or imperfections in our lives would not likely be classified as 'grievous'. But we still suffer as a result of them, and they prevent us from developing our full potential.

If we don't accept forgiveness, we have several options. We can justify our behaviour by blaming others. As previously stated, when we hear ourselves say: 'She/he makes me furious,' we are really placing blame on another soul for whatever has occurred. We are, in fact, admitting that we have handed over control of our lives to someone else. Our behaviour is justified. Alternatively, we can lower our standards by saying that 'everybody does it'. If we really care about living in the best possible way, when we hear ourselves make this remark, we suspect that it means *we* shouldn't be doing it! A third alternative is to swallow our feelings of guilt – and possibly develop an ulcer or other equally unpleasant physical reactions.

But if we accept God's forgiveness, we will be in the frame of mind where we can say, if we choose to, 'I'm sorry' with true sincerity to the person who has felt the hurt, *even if we did not intend to give hurt*. And here is where one can again think about the word 'heroism'. Most of us hate to face the person with whom we have had 'words', and it often requires real heroism to be able to ask that person what you have done to hurt them.

On one occasion I sensed a coldness in a fellow worker which had never been there before. We had always been the best of friends. Not being very heroic, it took me a couple of days before I could bring myself to ask her if there was anything wrong. Had I done anything to offend her? The answer was quite surprising. Apparently I had said something, in passing, which had been misinterpreted. After many apologies and assurances that I had, in no way, intended what she had thought, we were able to 'hug and make up'.

A spiritual law which was involved in this situation, and can form the basis for greater mutual understanding, is that of consultation. There are some people who are not ready to consult about relationships, and we cannot force them to do so. However, where two people respect the concept of consultation, it can be extremely helpful. It is, in fact, another spiritual law. Bahá'u'lláh said: '. . .Take ye counsel together in all matters, inasmuch as consultation is the lamp of guidance which leadeth the way, and is the bestower of understanding.'[7]

As we are all aware, the purpose of true consultation is to find a solution or the truth, and not to prove that one side is right. When we consider that we have been promised that 'understanding' will be the outcome of true consultation, one can easily see how helpful this would be in gaining a good relationship. It means that we can begin to understand what motivates our partner, or what he/she has understood from what we have said. This can often be quite the opposite of what we intended to convey.

The laws of consultation include the expressing of one's views with 'absolute freedom', but with 'courtesy, dignity, care and moderation', and that 'it is in no wise permissible for one to belittle the thought of another'.[8] Consultation should, if possible, be preceded by prayer, so that not only will the participants be in the right frame of mind to talk to each other, but the power of God will be invoked to assist them. 'No capacity is limited when led by the Spirit of God,' is a further promise made by 'Abdu'l-Bahá.[9]

In consultation we are not supposed to either give or receive hurt. As individuals, the challenge is quite clear. We do our best to neither give, nor accept any hurt. It may happen, however, in the heat of our own enthusiasm or our own convictions, we say something which is hurtful, however unintentional. A much prized attribute – sensitivity – is needed in perceiving if another person has been hurt by our remarks.

Sometimes we have hurt another person by giving them 'admonition or advice' (for their own good, of course!). There is a wonderful statement by 'Abdu'l-Bahá: 'Act in such a way that your heart may be free from hatred. Let not your heart be offended with any one. If someone commits an error and wrong toward you, you must instantly forgive him. Do not complain of others. Refrain from reprimanding them, and if you wish to give admonition or advice let it be offered in such a way that it will not burden the receiver.'[10]

It might be an interesting exercise to consider how one can offer 'admonition or advice' in such a way as to not 'burden the receiver'.

Before proceeding to the question of 'how we feel about other people and how we act toward them', it would no doubt be helpful to review what has been said.

Spiritual laws are like physical laws – immutable. There are many laws which have been revealed in the Writings of the Bahá'í Faith which help us to love. Spiritual law has been revealed to help us develop our potential and to achieve 'everlasting felicity'. The process is a gradual one, and one can learn, even through failure. There are two basic causes of disharmony – (1) *our reaction to what we see as another's judgment of ourself*, and (2) *our reaction towards another person as we judge their actions*. In both the instances our reaction can be both anger and hurt. The challenge is to 'act', rather than to simply 'react'.

In the case of (1), our reaction to what we see as another's judgment of ourself, the first conscious step towards utilizing spiritual laws in our desire to achieve love and harmony, is to accept God as our Judge. Next, we need to recognize, through the spiritual law of truthfulness, our own faults. If they are inconsequential, we can simply admit we've been wrong. If the problem is more serious, we may need to seek forgiveness from God. Through consultation we can begin to understand each other.

5

How we feel about others

How we feel about others is *extremely* important, because most often it is how we feel towards someone else which gets across. For example, even if we don't respond verbally when another person is attacking us, we are all very well aware of the 'cold treatment' in which one side remains aloof from the actual verbal battle, but punishes the opponent by a cold silence for the rest of the day. The response may, of course, be much less evident. It may not even be a conscious response. In other words, sometimes when we are deeply hurt, we may still try to say the right things, but the warmth and spontaneity is missing.

'Abdu'l-Bahá spoke about this: 'For to treat in a smooth, kindly manner one whom you consider as evil or an enemy is hypocrisy and this is not worthy or allowable. . . You must consider your enemies as your friends, look upon your evil-wishers as your well-wishers and treat them accordingly. Your love and kindness must be real. . . not merely forbearance, for forbearance, if not of the heart, is hypocrisy.'[1]

An example of how feelings get across was described in the book *Portals to Freedom* by Howard Colby Ives, a Unitarian Minister who met 'Abdu'l-Bahá on a number of occasions when He visited the United States. On one occasion 'Abdu'l-Bahá's interpretation of the words of Christ was quite different from the accepted one. When Howard Colby Ives stated that it wasn't possible to be sure of the meaning so many centuries later, 'Abdu'l-Bahá simply stated that it was possible. 'That I cannot believe', was the impatient response of the minister.

> I shall never forget the glance of outraged dignity the interpreter cast upon me. It was as though he would say: 'Who are you to contradict or even to question 'Abdu'l-Bahá!'.
> But not so did 'Abdu'l-Bahá look at me. How I thank God that it was not! He looked at me a long moment before He spoke. His calm beautiful eyes searched my soul with such love and understanding that all my momentary heat evaporated. He smiled as winningly as a lover smiles upon his beloved, and the arms of His spirit seemed to embrace me as He said softly that I should try my way and He would try His.

Howard Colby Ives goes on to compare it to the glance which Christ must have given to Peter following his three-fold denial. It couldn't have been the 'self-righteous, dignified look in the eyes of the interpreter', or Peter would never have come to be the great proclaimer of the Christian Faith. It must have been a similar 'expression of all-embracing love, forgiveness and understanding with which 'Abdu'l-Bahá calmed and soothed and assured my heart'.[2]

Before considering some of the spiritual laws which will help to ensure that the feeling which gets across to the other person is one of understanding and love, we should look at the other side of the coin. The other side of the coin is that we should not misinterpret the other person's intentions. Sometimes another person's harsh look can be from sore feet, or the fact that he or she didn't have their morning coffee!

It may be helpful to remind ourselves that all of the guidance and spiritual laws we are studying are directed towards us. We are told that *we* should be loving: obviously, we aren't going to tell others they should be more loving towards us. One other reminder is that despite all that we do, it might not be possible to bring about a loving relationship – or it might take a very long time to do so. We recall the story about 'Abdu'l-Bahá, or as He was often referred to by Bahá'u'lláh, the 'Master':

> When the Master came to Akka there lived there a certain man from Afghanistan, an austere and rigid Mussulman. To him the Master was a heretic. He felt and nourished a great enmity towards the Master, and roused up others against him. When opportunity offered in gatherings of the people, as in the Mosque, he denounced him with bitter words.

. . .And when he passed the Master on the street he was careful to hold his robe before his face that his sight might not be defiled.

Thus did the Afghan. The Master, however, did thus: The Afghan was poor and lived in a mosque; he was frequently in need of food and clothing. The Master sent him both. These he accepted, but without thanks. He fell sick. The Master took him a physician, food, medicine, money. These, also, he accepted; but as he held out one hand that the physician might take his pulse, with the other he held his cloak before his face that he might not look upon the Master. *For twenty-four years* the Master continued his kindnesses and the Afghan persisted in his enmity. Then at last one day the Afghan came to the Master's door, and fell down, penitent and weeping, at his feet.

'Forgive me, sir!' he cried. 'For twenty-four years I have done evil to you, for twenty-four years you have done good to me. Now I know that I have been in the wrong.'

The Master bade him rise, and they became friends.[3]

We now return to the theme of 'How we feel about others'. One of the most important spiritual laws we can consider is contained in the following two quotations from the Writings of Bahá'u'lláh:

The best beloved of all things in My sight is Justice. . .[4]

And if thine eyes be turned towards justice, choose thou for thy neighbour that which thou choosest for thyself.[5]

What do we choose for ourselves? To be understood: that what we did was because we believed it to be right; that the reason we lost our temper was because we had such a splitting headache; that we didn't really mean the unkind things we said last night in the heat of the battle; that when we are critical, it is because we want to see our partner as perfect; that our anger was because of our concern; that even where we have failed, our wish was to succeed. Bahá'u'lláh said that the first and foremost favour which God conferred upon man is 'the gift of understanding'.[6]

If we beamed this understanding, this 'choosing for others what we choose for ourselves' towards others, we might just see that people are not the incarnations of evil, bad temper, etc. any more than we are. We choose for ourselves that we be forgiven and the incident forgotten. We choose to be loved; to be treated courteously. Our choice is for someone to see our good qualities and ignore the (paltry few) bad ones.

'Abdu'l-Bahá was asked, 'How shall I overcome seeing the faults of others – recognizing the wrong in others?' He replied: 'I will tell you. Whenever you recognize the fault of another, think of yourself: What are my imperfections? – and try to remove them. Do this whenever you are tried through the words or deeds of others. Thus you will grow, become more perfect. You will overcome self, you will not even have time to think of the faults of others. . .'[7]

On the same subject, He said: 'To look always at the good and not at the bad. If a man has ten good qualities and one bad one, to look at the ten and forget the one; and if a man has ten bad qualities and one good one, to look at the one and forget the ten. . .'[8]

A letter written on behalf of the Guardian of the Bahá'í Faith, Shoghi Effendi, to a woman who was having marital difficulties, echoed this same guidance. (It should be noted that this advice could equally apply to a husband.) 'There are qualities in everyone which we can appreciate and admire, and for which we can love them; and perhaps, if you determine to think only of these qualities which your husband possesses, this will help to improve the situation. . . You should turn your thoughts away from the things which upset you, and constantly pray to Bahá'u'lláh to help you. Then you will find how that pure love, enkindled by God, which burns in the soul when we read and study the Teachings, will warm and heal, more than anything else.'[9]

There is a further implication in this statement; that one needs to not only pray to be assisted in the challenging goal of looking to another's good qualities, but that reading and studying the Teachings will 'warm and heal'.

So often, in the case of close relationships, one tends to take for granted the hundreds of good qualities in the other person, and instead, focuses on the annoying fact that he/she squeezes the top end of the toothpaste tube, leaves a tap dripping, takes forever to get ready to go out, or other relatively inconsequential (or not so inconsequential) habits. It might be an interesting exercise to make up two

lists over a period of a month: one which records
the number of times one complained about the
other person's faults, and the other the number of
times one expressed appreciation of that person's
good qualities. There is no doubt that most people
respond very positively to encouragement. This
must be why 'Abdu'l-Bahá said: 'Every one of the
friends should highly praise the other. . .'[10]

He also stated: 'Each sees in the other the
beauty of God reflected in the soul, and finding
this point of similarity, they are attracted to one
another in love.'[11] It may be difficult at times to
see the 'beauty of God' in another soul. One
individual likened it to a letter from a beloved
friend which has been carried around in one's
purse for months. The envelope may be coffee-
stained, dog-eared and grubby, but the letter is
quite possibly one's most precious possession. To
see beyond the exterior 'envelope' of another
human being may be one of our greatest chal-
lenges.

'Abdu'l-Bahá was able to do this. Someone
asked Him 'why it was that those who came from
His presence possessed a shining face. He said,
with that sublime smile and humble gesture of the
hands which once seen may never be forgotten,
that if it were so it must be because He saw in
every face the face of His Heavenly Father.'[12]

For centuries Christians have perceived the way
in which the life of Christ manifested the attributes of God, and this has helped them to gain

some small understanding of such attributes and to try to emulate them. Today we have many books about the lives of the Central Figures of the Bahá'í Faith, and we can gain a deeper understanding of these attributes by reading them. There is one story in particular about the life of Bahá'u'lláh in which the understanding of the motive of others is illustrated.

At a time of great persecution of the supporters of the Báb (Who was the Forerunner of Bahá'u'lláh). Bahá'u'lláh was taken by the authorities from His ancestral home to a terrible dungeon. He was led for miles, in the heat of an August sun, hatless, His hat (a sign of His position) thrown to the ground. An old woman picked up a rock to throw at Him. She begged the guards to slow down so she could throw the rock. Bahá'u'lláh said: 'Suffer not this woman to be disappointed. Deny her not what she regards as a meritorious act in the sight of God.'[13]

Bahá'u'lláh saw that the woman perceived her action as a defence of her love for Muḥammad against someone whom she thought was a threat to the Faith.

It is obvious that none of the things which those around us are doing can even vaguely compare with this particular act. But interesting parallels can be imagined in trying to perceive the good motives which may have been behind the hurtful acts of another person. For example, someone's anger at your late arrival may be an indication of that person's love and concern that something might have happened to you. We know that we can never hope to attain, even to the tiniest degree, the understanding and compassion which Bahá'u'lláh evinced, but such stories give us an inkling of what 'understanding' really means.

There is another very helpful concept in developing loving relations and in not permitting the faults of others to prevent us from radiating the loving, spiritual part of our natures. Bahá'u'lláh states: 'If any differences arise amongst you, behold Me standing before your face, and overlook the faults of one another for My name's sake, and as a token of your love for My manifest and resplendent Cause.'[14]

Although we cannot visualize the Manifestation of God, Bahá'u'lláh, we can perhaps visualize 'Abdu'l-Bahá, the true Exemplar of all the spiritual qualities which Bahá'u'lláh manifested. Could we see His face before us and scream out in anger at another human being? Of course not. But it wouldn't be a case of not reacting in anger out of fear of 'Abdu'l-Bahá's displeasure, or because we wouldn't wish to offend Him. It would seem more likely that if we really felt the perfect love and understanding of 'Abdu'l-Bahá, our response would have to be one which reflected that love and understanding.

It is important that when there is a feeling of division and disunity, we strive conscientiously to find the spiritual law which *we* (not the other person) are breaking. Are we accepting hurt? Are we looking at someone else's faults? We may not always be able to effect a perfect reconciliation, but at least we will have done all that is possible. In addition to striving to improve our attitude towards others, there are spiritual laws with which we are no doubt familiar, dealing directly with how we act towards others.

6

How we act towards others

There are a great many spiritual laws and words of guidance in the Writings which have been bountifully revealed to us to assist us in learning how to love. A few of these will be included. However, the reader is cautioned that a casual reading of them will not be sufficient to reveal the depths of their meaning. Bahá'u'lláh said: 'Immerse yourselves in the ocean of My words, that ye may unravel its secrets, and discover all the pearls of wisdom that lie hid in its depths.'[1] He further stated that 'One hour's reflection is preferable to seventy years of pious worship.'[2]

It is therefore suggested that all the quotations included in this brief presentation (and in other Writings of the Faith) should be reflected upon to gain the 'pearls of wisdom' which lie hidden in their depths.

Bahá'u'lláh spoke very strongly about the attribute of courtesy. He said: 'O people of God! I exhort you to courtesy. Courtesy is, in the primary station, the Lord of all virtues. Blessed is he who is illumined with the light of courtesy, and is adorned with the mantle of uprightness! He who is endowed with courtesy is endowed with a great station.'[3]

When Bahá'u'lláh designates courtesy, in the primary station, as 'the lord of all virtues', could it mean that every act we perform, unless it is clothed in the garment of courtesy, is an imperfect act?

The more that we reflect on the idea of courtesy, in its primary station, as 'the Lord of all virtues', the greater depths we will plumb in the meaning of this highly-praised attribute. A few thoughts on the subject follow.

It would seem obvious that one of the most important aspects of courtesy is the art of listening. This is of particular importance if we are engaged in consultation. Very often the participants are not really listening to what is being said, but are instead thinking about the point they wish to make. This means that there is no real communication. It is also true of ordinary conversations between two people, particularly where the situation is strained. How can we really make contact with another human being if we do not have the courtesy not only to hear what they are saying, but to make an effort to understand?

Courtesy comes into play in so many facets of life. The person who is always on time shows great consideration for the other person's busy schedule. Courtesy is involved in the way in which we treat those who are performing a service for us, whether at home, in a store, or a garage. It is reflected even in the relatively simple, everyday acts we perform, such as the serving of a meal. A simple meal served graciously is enjoyed far more than a banquet presented by a surly waiter. There is even the need for courtesy in the giving and receiving of gifts. How disappointing it is to present a gift, perhaps one we have spent a great deal of time in finding, and have the recipient hardly say 'thank you'. In the carrying out of allocated tasks, courtesy is essential. Every mother knows how unpleasant it can be if the child, in fulfilling his task of washing dishes, does so with a disgruntled, ungracious attitude. Perhaps our attitude towards our own responsibilities (some of which may be rather tiresome or boring) should be examined. There are innumerable ways in which courtesy needs to become an integral part of our whole way of life.

It can be easy to slip into a 'take it for granted' attitude in which even the simple courtesies of 'please', 'thank you', 'would you kindly', are forgotten. Some years ago, a friend who was having marital difficulties admitted that when her husband returned from work, she would barely greet him, and customarily, would simply hand him one of the younger children (they had six) to look after while she finished preparing supper. It suddenly occurred to her one day that if a friend arrived at the door, she would immediately greet the friend warmly, ask after her health, and generally make that person feel wanted and loved. She decided to try this with her husband. The results were very encouraging.

In training our children in the art of courtesy, example is of far greater influence than innumerable reminders that they must say 'please' and 'thank you'. In fact, example is the greatest gift we can give to our offspring. (This theme would require another book to explore!) Very often children have the annoying habit of interrupting adults when they are talking. It is not infrequently that we see parents either ignore the child or speak very sharply, reminding the youngster (in a not-too-courteous fashion) that it is impolite to interrupt. My mother-in-law had a very courteous way of dealing with this problem. She would simply place her hand on the shoulder or hand of the child, acknowledging the child's presence. This would reassure the youngster that when there was a break in the conversation, she would respond.

Another aspect of courtesy is contained in what is termed the 'Marriage Tablet', in the words: 'Take counsel together in secret.' How many times do we hear the faults of people's spouses (or children) being bruited publicly, quite often even in their presence. There is a great deal to be said about the oriental custom of 'face saving'.

One very perceptive statement about courtesy was included in the play *Pygmalion*, later made into the musical *My Fair Lady*. Near the end of the play, Eliza Doolittle makes a comparison between the way she was treated by Professor Higgins (very rudely) and Colonel Pickering. She said that the latter treated her like a lady. Even the first day she arrived, he addressed her as 'Miss Doolittle' and asked her kindly to sit down. She summed up her comments by saying that the difference between a flower girl and a lady is really in the way she is treated.

Perhaps this was the secret behind the story, mentioned earlier, in which those who left the presence of 'Abdu'l-Bahá emerged with a shining face, and that 'Abdu'l-Bahá attributed this to the fact that He had seen in 'every face the face of His Heavenly Father'.

We don't usually realize that insisting on our own will or seeking an advantage over another person is an aspect of discourtesy. But isn't it? Bahá'u'lláh couples such guidance with a rather obvious directive about courtesy. He said: '. . .no man should enter the house of his friend save at his friend's pleasure, nor lay hands upon his treasures nor prefer his own will to his friend's, and in no wise seek an advantage over him. . .'[4]

Let us now look at another spiritual law which relates how we speak to and about each other.

These quotations deal with the subject of the tongue, and are from the Writings of Bahá'u'lláh:

A kindly tongue is the lodestone of the hearts of men. It is the bread of the spirit, it clotheth the words with meaning, it is the fountain of the light of wisdom and understanding.[5]

. . .the tongue is a smouldering fire, and excess of speech a deadly poison. Material fire consumeth the body, whereas the fire of the tongue devoureth both heart and soul. The force of the former lasteth but for a time, whilst the effects of the latter endureth a century.'[6]

['Abdu'l-Bahá said:] '. . .Stories repeated about others are seldom good. A silent tongue is safest. Even good may be harmful if spoken at the wrong time or to the wrong person.'[7]

What a powerful influence words have on us from our earliest childhood! It is interesting that the concept of a 'magnet' (lodestone) is used both in relation to a 'kindly tongue' and in the quotation on love itself: 'In the world of existence there is no more powerful magnet than the magnet of love.'[8] There is no doubt that we are repelled by harsh words and hatred; and that kindliness of speech and a loving nature attract us in the same way that iron filings fly upwards to a magnet. This spiritual law is self-evident.

Where problems exist in our relationship to another person, perhaps it would be helpful to consciously examine whether our speech could be characterized by the words 'a kindly tongue' or whether it more closely resembles a 'smouldering fire'.

We are sometimes unaware of how we sound to others. The teenage children of one couple tape-recorded a heated argument of their parents, and then played it back to them. Needless to say, the parents were not only shocked by the harsh sound of their voices; they were deeply embarrassed!

The second quotation above might seem to be exaggerated if we were not aware of the effect which verbal abuse has on the developing nature of a child over a period of time; and how this same kind of verbal abuse is often repeated when that child grows up and becomes a parent. 'Abdu'l-Bahá clearly stated:

> Whensoever a mother seeth that her child hath done well, let her praise and applaud him and cheer his heart; and if the slightest undesirable trait should manifest itself, let her counsel the child and punish him, and use means based on reason, even a slight verbal chastisement should this be necessary. It is not, however, permissible to strike a child, or vilify him, for the child's character will be totally perverted if he be subjected to blows or verbal abuse.[9]

Bahá'u'lláh said we should speak primarily with words as 'mild as milk' so that others would attain their ultimate goal – 'the station of true understanding and nobility':

> One word may be likened unto fire, another unto light, and the influence which both exert is manifest in the world. Therefore an enlightened man of wisdom should primarily speak with words as mild as milk, that the children of men may be nurtured and

edified thereby and may attain the ultimate goal of human existence which is the station of true understanding and nobility.[10]

One spiritual law which describes in a few words what should be our relationship to others, was stated by 'Abdu'l-Bahá: 'Life in man should be like a flame, warming all with whom it comes in contact.'[11]

In case we become too overwhelmed by recognition of the spiritual laws which we have not been able to observe, it would be helpful to recall the words written on behalf of Shoghi Effendi:

We must not only be patient with others, infinitely patient!, but also with our own poor selves, remembering that even the Prophets of God sometimes got tired and cried out in despair![12]

There are, of course, many other words of guidance which we may study in our efforts to become loving human beings. The following statement of Bahá'u'lláh really sums up the concept of spiritual law:

True liberty consisteth in man's submission unto My commandments, little as ye know it.[13]

This statement of Bahá'u'lláh becomes very clear when we think about love. We have only to recall the feeling of joyousness when we feel love – the sense of release – the wonderful ability to be able to tease each other without fear of hurt. On the other hand, when we are angry, we are held, as it were, in a vise. We are no longer creative, helpful or able to even think in a logical manner. It is no wonder that 'Abdu'l-Bahá said: 'Order your lives in accordance with the first principle of the divine teaching, which is love.'[14]

7

Dependence on love

A great deal has been said about the importance of love. Most of us are only too conscious of how dependent we can become on the
feeling that we are loved by another person. When
we do not feel that love, we can become very
depressed. We may find ourselves unable to
respond to life in the same positive way we do
when we are conscious of being loved. And, of
course, it becomes a vicious circle. The more we
feel unloved, the less capable we are of showing
love and concern for the other person and, on the
other hand, the less he/she is able to show love to
us.

There will always be times in any relationship
when one side or the other is not loving. If it is
only for a brief period of time, and the basic love
is strong, each can overcome whatever hurt is felt.
However, all too often each partner stores up

the hurt feelings, or responds in anger, and the relationship is gradually eroded.

It is perfectly natural to feel a sense of joy when one feels love. However, if our sense of well-being and self-worth is largely dependent on the approval of another individual, we are, in a sense, placing that person in the position of God. We are disregarding one of the most important spiritual laws – that of looking to God as our Judge. We are also not accepting the powerful gift of His love which can change the feeling of despair into one of hope. We are reminded of the fact that we have been created out of the love of God in the following words of Bahá'u'lláh:

> O Son of Man! Veiled in My immemorial being and in the ancient eternity of My essence, I knew My love for thee; therefore I created thee, have engraved on thee Mine image and revealed to thee My beauty.[1]

I believe that we need to develop as a 'whole' person before we are capable of loving another individual. We have to recognize that we have been created by God, that we have the potential of manifesting wonderful qualities, and that we have been promised the help of God in attaining these attributes. It is axiomatic that we must take responsibility for our own development and for the effect we have on others.

It is very important to realize the unfailing love which God has for us. When we are able to feel this love we are able to respond to life in a joyous, creative and tranquil manner. In other words, we are able to manifest the qualities which are latent within us. Someone's bad humour may temporarily cause us to be ruffled, but if we are sustained by the strengthening power which comes from the love of God, our own positive feelings can usually keep us from being seriously disturbed.

I suggest that we need to perceive this love on both a *thoughtful* (or one might say an intellectual) level and on an *emotional* level. If we think about the statement of Bahá'u'lláh that we were created out of God's love for us, this truth becomes clear when we realize that He has given us, potentially, His own attributes – love, forgiveness, creativity, joy, and understanding. What greater proof of love than to realize that God has engraved these holy attributes upon our inmost true selves!

It becomes even more clear when we accept the fact that God has enabled us to acquire these hidden attributes. How? By revealing to us His beauty in the person of His Manifestation. These Manifestations have appeared to mankind down through the ages. At this point in time it is through the Manifestation of God, Bahá'u'lláh, and through His Teachings, that we can learn to manifest all of our potential attributes. 'The Purpose of the one true God, exalted be His glory, in revealing Himself unto men is to lay bare those gems that lie hidden within the mine of their true and inmost selves.'[2]

Sometimes the desirable attributes, 'the gems', are completely hidden. A graphic example of the statement that there is within every human being the potential of reflecting God-like qualities, and that through the power of God these qualities may be developed, is the story repeated so many times at an AA meeting. Most of us are familiar with the tale of the person who has sunk to the lowest depths and who, to outward appearances, has no desirable human qualities. Yet when the person recognizes his own powerlessness and the power of God (or however he wishes to express the concept), he can be transformed into a useful, joyous, and loved member of human society. If we are truly conscious that these qualities are latent within us, a feeling of self-worth can be nurtured. However, we need to feel the love of God.

This can only come about if the love is reciprocal. Think back to that wonderful moment when you were first 'in love'. There may have been times when someone has fallen in love with you, but unless you feel love in return, it has no meaning. When you love in return, the world is transformed.

There are times, however, even if you are 'in love', that you become angry. At such moments, you do not feel the other person's love. It is the same way with a child. A youngster, in a rage, may storm off into his room saying, 'I hate you, Mommy!' The mother still loves the child, but her love cannot reach him. It is exactly the same way with the love of God for his creatures. If we do not love God in return, we cannot feel His love. *But God continues to love us.* When we are able to feel this love, we feel a tremendous sense of joy. It is the 'spirit of life'. In the words of Bahá'u'lláh:

> O Son of Man! I loved thy creation, hence I created thee. Wherefore, do thou love Me, that I may name thy name and fill thy soul with the spirit of life.[3]

Today there is a lot of talk about 'unconditional' love. In one way, we could say that the love of God for His creatures is 'unconditional'. It is always there. In another sense, however, being able to actually *feel* the love of God is conditional upon certain things. Bahá'u'lláh said that the love of God would only reach us if we loved Him.

> O Son of Being! Love Me, that I may love thee. If thou lovest Me not, My love can in no wise reach thee. Know this, O servant.[4]

How can we love God? It would take another booklet to talk about this subject in depth, but let us look briefly at three ways. The first was mentioned by 'Abdu'l-Bahá in *Portals to Freedom* when someone asked Him how one could love God. 'Dost thou desire to love God? Love thy fellow men, for in them ye see the image and likeness of God.'[5] It is obvious that we really want to love our fellow men. We know that the need to give and receive love is a basic truth. It is not only basic in the very personal sense, but even in the sense of wishing to live in harmony with those not closely related to us. There is probably nothing which makes us more unhappy than to be at odds with each other. At the same time, nothing makes us feel happier than to feel love. It is certain that the very efforts we make to be obedient to the spiritual law to 'love thy fellow men' will help us to feel a sense of the love of God.

Being obedient to the laws of God is, in fact, a second way in which we practice love towards our Creator. Bahá'u'lláh said: 'Observe My commandments, for the love of My beauty.'[6] The way in which we strive to obey whatever laws and guidance have been laid down by this Messenger of God indicates the measure of our love for God.

A third way is through prayer – and here is where we perceive the love of God on an emotional level. It is when we pray that we are able to make a connection with the spirit of love which surrounds us. 'Abdu'l-Bahá said, 'The greatest happiness for a lover is to converse with his beloved, and the greatest gift for a seeker is to become familiar with the object of his longing.'[7] He also said: 'Draw nigh unto God and persevere in [thy] communion with [or prayer to] thy Lord, so that the fire of God's love may glow more luminously in thy heart. . .'[8] If we wish to feel the love of God, it would therefore seem only natural that we should pray.

It is, in fact, an important spiritual law. 'Supplication to God at morn and eve is conducive to the joy of hearts and prayer causes spirituality and fragrance. Thou shouldst necessarily continue therein.'[9]

Are there not spiritual laws in prayers? If a prayer is revealed by a Manifestation of God, surely we may expect to receive what we ask for – unless, for example, 'healing' would cause further problems:

Make my heart to overflow with love for Thy creatures. . .

. . .Refresh and gladden my spirit. . .

. . .at the hour of dawn my drooping soul is refreshed and strengthened in remembrance of Thy beauty and perfection. . .

Let Thine everlasting melodies breathe tranquillity on me. . .

Illumine the eyes, gladden the hearts with abiding joy. . .[10]

These are just a few excerpts from the prayers of Bahá'u'lláh and 'Abdu'l-Bahá which constitute requests for love, tranquillity and joy – all of which are needed if we want to feel love for each other. And if we pray for them, should we not expect to feel these qualities? Then why does this feeling of love and joy often elude us?

If prayer is only carried out as a duty, it is like visiting a sick friend out of a sense of duty only. It does neither one any good. But there are other reasons which can prevent us from feeling the sense of tranquillity, joy or love we long for. Sometimes it is because our minds are filled with thoughts of a thousand other things. Huston

Smith, in his book *The Religions of Man* (p.52) tells an amusing story about the mind.

> The motions of the average mind, say the Hindus, are about as purposeful and orderly as those of a crazed monkey cavorting about its cage. Nay, more, like the prancings of a drunk, crazed monkey. Even so we have not conveyed its full restlessness; the mind is like a drunk, crazed monkey that has St. Vitus' dance. If we are to be truly accurate to its frenzy we must go a final step; it is like a drunk, crazed monkey with St. Vitus' dance who has just been stung by a wasp.

So it is quite understandable that true prayer is elusive. One needs to pray with 'concentrated attention' for the prayer to unite us with the Spirit of God. Bahá'u'lláh in *The Seven Valleys* quotes from the mystics: 'A servant is drawn unto Me in prayer until I answer him. . .'[11] Is it possible that we sometimes pray, and do not pray long enough, or with a great enough sense of detachment, to feel the reply?

In this respect, it might be helpful to bear in mind the words of 'Abdu'l-Bahá: 'The highest and most elevating state is the state of prayer. Prayer is communion with God. . . . *its efficacy is conditional* upon the freedom of the heart from extraneous suggestions and mundane thoughts. The worshipper must pray with a detached spirit, unconditional surrender of the will, concentrated attention and a magnetic spiritual passion. . .'[12]

It is not easy to detach oneself from one's surroundings or one's own particular problems in life in order to pray in this way – and possibly even harder to give 'concentrated attention'. But almost certainly the rewards of the spirit are commensurate with the efforts made to reach this pinnacle of detachment.

Perhaps one of the greatest gifts we will receive concerning the power of prayer is our experience during the Fast. In these days of instant gratification, we suddenly find ourselves without even the comfort of a cup of coffee. We find, in fact, that there is nowhere to which we can turn. . . except God. We are solely reliant on prayer. When we pray with sincerity and urgency, we find that we are able to overcome what might be a sense of irritability, deprived as we are of normal sustenance. A sense of joy will often replace those feelings.

In everyday life all of us may sometimes feel depressed, angry, discouraged. When we realize the power which is given to us through prayer, we can not only be released from those negative feelings, but we can receive inspiration and courage in other aspects of our existence. It is at this point that the statement, 'Yet to be poor in all save God is a wondrous gift'[13] can become the reality of our lives.

We started off this chapter by talking about the dependence one can sometimes feel on the love of another person in order to feel 'whole'. We have tried to illustrate that this feeling of 'wholeness' has to first come from a recognition that we were created by God, and that such qualities as tranquillity, joy and love are potentially within us. In order to manifest them, we need to be obedient to His spiritual laws and to be conscious of God's love. When we are able to feel this love, especially through prayer, we are better able to withstand the trials and tests which are often a part of our relationships with those around us, and sometimes with the one whom we hold most dear.

8

Reinforcement is needed

Before we talk about reinforcement, let us briefly review what has been said concerning the statement, 'The most important feat in this day is harmony and agreement.'

Most people find that the achievement of love is, indeed, a 'feat', and one which is difficult to achieve. The premise has been made that by following spiritual laws we can reach our goal. It was suggested that there are two basic factors which prevent us from loving, both of which cause a negative reaction. The first is the way we think others feel about us. The second is the way we feel about, and act towards, others.

Concerning the question of how we think others feel about us, if we observe the law that God is our judge, and not our fellow man, we are released from the necessity of reacting to negative comments. However, a proviso was included that we should be 'unmoved by praise or *false* accusations'. The spiritual law of truthfulness has to be invoked in order to determine the truth of the accusations, and where appropriate, admission of one's faults. The laws of forgiveness, through prayer, consultation with the other party, and 'acting' rather than 'reacting' were included as a means of overcoming this aspect of what prevents us from loving.

In examining the way we feel about others, and act towards them, it was stressed that it is usually what we feel which gets across. Attention was drawn to the need to choose for others what we choose for ourselves – particularly as it relates to our judgment of them. The spiritual law of looking to the good qualities of another instead of their faults was stated, as was the sublime quality of 'Abdu'l-Bahá to see in 'every face the face of His Heavenly Father'.

In looking at the second aspect of our relationship to others, how we act towards them, two laws in particular were explored; that of courtesy and of the tongue.

Finally, the question of our dependence on the love of another person in order to feel 'whole' was raised, and the premise set forth that we need to recognize that the qualities of 'wholeness' have already been placed within us by God. In order to manifest them, we need to be obedient to His laws and to actually feel His love through prayer. This love gives us the capacity to withstand the trials and difficulties which are often part of a relationship.

We now examine the need for reinforcement. The five points which will be made were taken from a letter (from the Hands of the Cause in the Holy Land, 30 May 1956, which was written to the Hands of the Cause in the United States on behalf of the Guardian). This letter was actually in relation to teaching, and it stated that one must '*study* deeply the Divine Word, imbibe its life-giving waters, and feast upon its glorious teachings. He should then *meditate* on the import of the Word, and finding its spiritual depth, *pray* for guidance and assistance. But most important, after prayer is *action*. . . *Perseverance* in action is essential. . .'

These five points are extremely important in our efforts to become loving individuals.

Concerning the first point, although many of the 'Divine Words' will already be familiar to many readers, we need reinforcement to ensure that they are constantly in our minds, and directing both our feelings and our actions. Perhaps this is why Bahá'u'lláh said: 'Chant (or recite) the words of God every morning and evening. The one who neglects this has not been faithful to the Covenant of God and His agreement.'[1] 'Abdu'l-Bahá also commanded us to '. . .investigate and study the Holy Scriptures word by word so that you may attain knowledge of the mysteries hidden therein. Be not satisfied with words, but seek to understand the spiritual meanings hidden in the heart of the words. . .'[2]

The second point was that one must meditate on the import of the Word. 'Abdu'l-Bahá said: 'The meditative faculty is akin to the mirror; if you put it before earthly objects it will reflect them. Therefore if the spirit of man is contemplating earthly subjects he will be informed of these. But if you turn the mirror of your spirits heavenwards . . . the rays of the Sun of Reality will be reflected in your hearts, and the virtues of the Kingdom will be obtained.'[3] He goes on to say that through meditation 'we may discover the secrets of the Kingdom'. It is unquestionably true that if we meditate on, for example, the quotations on truthfulness, whole new vistas of meaning of the word will come to our minds.

The third point concerns prayer. 'Supplication to God at morn and eve is conducive to the joy of hearts and prayer causes spirituality and fragrance. Thou shouldst necessarily continue therein.'[4] Try it sometime. There are times when one can feel sad or depressed for no apparent reason. In a beautiful tribute paid to the Greatest Holy Leaf (the beloved Sister of 'Abdu'l-Bahá) it was stated, 'When you went to her unsatisfied and restless you discovered that your unrest and discontent were really homelessness of spirit.' Is this not one of the prime purposes of prayer – to bring us to the true 'home' of the spirit – the sense of the presence of

God? The wonderful fact is that we are not alone. As implied earlier, the concept of 'my powerlessness and Thy Might' from the obligatory noonday prayer,[5] contains the key to the unlocking of our potential.

It may seem a daunting task to try and observe all the spiritual laws – to try to be forgiving when we feel desperately hurt, or to try to see good qualities when we are overwhelmed by the perception of bad ones. But we are promised: 'Thou art He Who changeth through His bidding abasement into glory, and weakness into strength, and powerlessness into might, and fear into calm, and doubt into certainty. . .'[6]

The fourth point concerns action. In the original letter it, of course, had to do with teaching. In adapting these thoughts to the concept of achieving love, we need to look at the idea of action with new eyes. One usually connects the idea of action with physical movement or action through words. Often this is not action at all, but reaction. In the case of a quarrel, reaction causes the two conflicting parties to speak ever more loudly, and sometimes actually come to blows! Some of our greatest actions take the form of reflection or meditation on the spiritual laws long before there is any sign of dissension. However, if it looks as if a quarrel is about to erupt, it is quite possible that the best action one can take is to either defuse the potential bomb by admitting we were wrong, or to hold one's tongue, and, as mentioned earlier, to inwardly pray for strength and tranquillity. If a matter needs to be discussed, it is almost impossible to do so in the heat of battle. A part of action is also facing up to the fact that there are problems, and that through striving to follow the spiritual laws of God they can be resolved.

The final point indicates that perseverance in action is essential. There is no doubt that in trying to observe the spiritual laws, we will fail innumerable times. But we must persevere. If each failure can be considered as a learning experience, we will be able to utilize it, and gradually acquire those much sought-after spiritual qualities which will enable us to 'live in everlasting felicity'.

We close with a portion of one of 'Abdu'l-Bahá's prayers which indicate the lofty heights He perceived as possible for mankind:

> Day and night I pray to Heaven for you that strength may be yours, and that, one and all, you may participate in the blessings of Bahá'u'lláh, and enter into the Kingdom.
>
> I supplicate that you may become as new beings illumined with the Divine Light . . . and that from one end of Europe to the other the knowledge of the love of God may spread.
>
> May this boundless love so fill your hearts and minds that sadness may find no room to enter.
>
> May your eyes be opened to see the signs of the Kingdom of God, and may your ears be unstopped so that you may hear with a perfect understanding the heavenly Proclamation sounding in your midst.
>
> May your souls receive help and comfort, and,

being so strengthened, may they be enabled to live in accordance with the teachings of Bahá'u'lláh.

I pray for each and all that you may be as flames of love in the world, and that the brightness of your light and the warmth of your affection may reach the heart of every sad and sorrowing child of God.[7]

References

The following abbreviations are used:

AB   *'Abdu'l-Bahá, The Centre of the Covenant of Bahá'u'lláh.* H.M. Balyuzi. Oxford: George Ronald, 1971.

ADJ   *The Advent of Divine Justice.* Shoghi Effendi. Wilmette: Bahá'í Publishing Trust, 1969.

AHW   *Hidden Words* (Arabic). Bahá'u'lláh. Various editions.

BNE   *Bahá'u'lláh and the New Era.* J.E. Esslemont. Wilmette: Bahá'í Publishing Trust, 1980.

BKG   *Bahá'u'lláh, The King of Glory.* H.M. Balyuzi. Oxford: George Ronald, 1980.

BM&FL   *Bahá'í Marriage and Family Life.* National Spiritual Assembly of the Bahá'ís of Canada, 1983.

BP   *Bahá'í Prayers.* Wilmette: Bahá'í Publishing Trust, 1982.

BWF   *Bahá'í World Faith*. Wilmette: Bahá'í
       Publishing Trust, 1956.

CON   *Consultation: A Compilation*. Research
       Department of the Universal House of
       Justice. Various editions.

DAL   *The Divine Art of Living*. M.H. Paine.
       Wilmette: Bahá'í Publishing Trust,
       1960.

DU'Á   *Du-á = On Wings of Prayer*. Ruth
       Moffett, rev. Keven Brown. Nature-
       graph, 1984.

GWB   *Gleanings from the Writings of
       Bahá'u'lláh*. Bahá'u'lláh. Wilmette:
       Bahá'í Publishing Trust, 1951.

KA   *The Kitáb-i-Aqdas*. Bahá'u'lláh. Haifa:
       Bahá'í World Centre, 1993.

PBL   *The Pattern of Bahá'í Life*. London:
       Bahá'í Publishing Trust, 1970.

PHW   *Hidden Words* (Persian). Bahá'u'lláh.
       Various editions.

PTF   *Portals to Freedom*. H.C. Ives.
       Oxford: George Ronald, 1976.

PBM   'Preserving Bahá'í Marriages'. Research
       Department of the Universal House of
       Justice, 1990.

SV   *The Seven Valleys*. Bahá'u'lláh. Various
       editions.

SWAB   *Selections from the Writings of 'Abdu'l-
       Bahá*. Haifa: Bahá'í World Centre,
       1978.

TB   *Tablets of Bahá'u'lláh Revealed after the Kitáb-i-Aqdas.* Haifa: Bahá'í World Centre, 1978.

References to the *Kitáb-i-Aqdas* are by paragraph number; to *Gleanings from the Writings of Bahá'u'lláh* by section number; and to the *Hidden Words* by verse number. Other references are to page numbers unless otherwise indicated.

1 The most important feat
  1 BWF 408
  2 BL 56
  3 PBL 53

3 Spiritual law and physical law
  1 GWB CX
  2 GWB CXXXIII
  3 KA 3
  4 KA 3

4 What we think others feel about us
  1 GWB CXIV
  2 DAL 9
 ·3 PBL 41
  4 GWB XXVII
  5 ADJ 20
  6 BP 82–3
  7 CON no. I

8 Ibid. no. 10

9 DAL 46

10 DAL 118–9

5 How we feel about others

1 BNE 93

2 PTF 37–8

3 Phelps, M.H., *Abbas Effendi, His Life and Teachings*, in AB 101

4 AHW 2

5 TB 64

6 GWB XCV

7 BM&FL no. 137

8 BNE 94

9 PBM 5

10 CON no. 16

11 PBL 33

12 PTF 46

13 BKG 78

14 GWB CXLVI

6 How we act towards others

1 DAL 41

2 DAL 39

3 PBL 26

4 PHW 43

5 GWB CXXXII

6 PBL 35

7 BM&FL no. 112

8 PBL 53

9 SWAB 125

10 TB 173
11 PBL 53
12 BM&FL no. 127
13 KA 125
14 PBL 56

7 Dependence on love
1 AHW 3
2 GWB CXXXII
3 AHW 4
4 AHW 5
5 PTF 46
6 KA 4
7 DAL 27
8 DAL 28
9 DAL 33
10 BP 31, 152, 32, 143, 102
11 SV 22
12 DU'Á 60
13 AHW 51

8 Reinforcement is needed
1 DAL 40
2 Ibid.
3 DAL 39
4 DAL 33
5 BP 4
6 DAL 32
7 DAL 30–31